Who Let the Dads Out?

a selection

of some of the

Best of Dad Blogging

Edited by Tom Briggs

Published in 2011 by Dotterel Press
ISBN: 978-0-9562869-5-6

Copyright © Introduction & Your Shout Dylan: Tom Briggs
Other material Copyright © individual authors

First Edition

The authors assert their moral rights under the Copyright, Designs and Patents Act 1988 to be identified as the authors of this work.

A catalogue record of this work is available from the British Library

The contents are entirely works of fiction. The names, characters, incidents and locations portrayed are the work of the various authors' imaginations. Any resemblance to actual persons, living or dead, events or localities is unintentional and entirely fictitious.

All rights reserved. No part of this publication may be reproduced, stored in a retrieval system, or transmitted, in any form or by any means, electronic, mechanical, photocopying, recording or otherwise without the prior permission of the publisher.

This book is sold subject to the condition that it shall not, by way of trade or otherwise, be lent, re-sold, hired out or otherwise circulated without the prior permission of the publisher in any form of binding or cover other than that in which it is published and without a similar condition being imposed on the subsequent purchaser.

Welcome...

Welcome, dear reader, to what we believe is a first. An anthology of blogs written exclusively by dads*.

The parent blogging community seems to be only rivalled by the universe itself for its inherent ability to expand at an incredible rate. It's a wonderful place to be in but it has to be said that those of us with a Y chromosome are somewhat in the minority. So it was that, around a year after starting my own blog, I somehow got shortlisted for a MAD Blog Award.

At the ceremony, I bumped into well-known dad blogger and thoroughly bloody nice chap, Tim Atkinson. Before the ceremony started, we got chatting and the idea for this very book came up. To cut a very long story short, it was a win-win situation – I won my award and we decided to use and abuse Tim's publishing experience to do this book. Obviously.

So here it is: a group of us have provided some of our favourite blog posts. There is no particular order to what follows, just an insight into the kind of thing that us dad bloggers populate the internet with. Oh, and we threw this book together inside a fortnight – please forgive the lack of ceremony! We hope you like what you see and, if you're a father who has a thing or two to say, that you'll join us in the blogosphere. Enjoy!

Tom Briggs, Editor
Blogger, Diary of the Dad

* We're not absolutely sure it's a first, mind, so don't quote us on this!

The Blog Up North

I am Him Up North, and the author of The Blog Up North. I live in Yorkshire, UK, with my wife (Her Up North) and my two boys (Wunderkind and Moppet). The Blog Up North is my space to write about anything and everything of interest to me: parenting, education, music to name but a few.

21 January 2011

Here is the news: I didn't have a dad either

Celebrity scandal came from an unlikely source this week. BBC journalist and news presenter Justin Webb admitted that he was the son of a former BBC news reader, Peter Woods, born after Woods had an affair with Webb's mother in the early 60s. Okay, so it's not right up there with Jordan and Alex, but the finer detail caught my attention.

Webb revealed he felt he had spent his formative years without a "proper" father. He knew who his father was, saw him on television, but at the same time was starkly aware that this man from whom he had inherited 50% of his chromosomes had a life and a family elsewhere. Apart from one brief encounter during infancy, father and son never met face to face.

While Justin Webb's mother eventually married (and Justin took his stepfather's surname), Webb claims to have missed something. He feels it has informed his own attitudes to fatherhood, and his revelations (coming now that his parents are dead) have been prompted by his own children asking about his past.

All this chimes very loudly with me.

I was the product of an affair too. My mother was unmarried, my father (a friend of the family) married to someone else. The difference between my story and Webb's is that my mother never married after I was born. She brought me up with the help and support of HER mum. This was about ten years after Justin Webb was born and attitudes had not become much more enlightened (although Webb's mother was dismissed from her job for becoming pregnant).

My father tried to deny my existence and fought shy of supporting my mum financially. She took him to court and won. My battle was in my head, and in the playground. As a child I felt... different. Around other children and their families, at school concerts, parents evenings, sports days, I was the one with just my mum there.

It felt awkward when school work turned to the subject of what our dads did for a job. Children, being children, noticed my situation, of course. And children, being children, would ask, with all the subtlety of a wrecking ball, "why haven't you got a dad?" "Because I haven't," was the usual, somewhat feeble reply.

I remember my mother giving me the same answer. I remember only one occasion asking her who my father was. When she told me I didn't believe her. As time went by and I got older I felt the awkwardness easing a bit. Perhaps growing older was putting some distance between me and the circumstances of my birth, diluting the essence of it. At the same time I felt mature enough to confront the gaps in my history and ask some questions.

When I was 18, I met my father for the only time I can remember. He had moved back to Canada but was over in Britain to see his sons by his marriage. He was staying with a mutual friend of my mum and we all arranged to meet in a local pub. When we arrived, he had one of his sons in tow. His kids didn't know about me and it was abundantly clear they weren't about to find out. My dad barely acknowledged me all evening. Had I wanted I could have pulled the pin and blown the lid off, but I didn't. It was all I needed to know. It closed a chapter.

Now I'm a father I wonder if my lack of a paternal influence has affected my own parenting. To be honest I think it made me a paternal blank slate. No point of reference nor embedded skills. I don't know what works, so I work it out myself (with, of course, everything I learned from my mum). My own boys noticed early on the lack of symmetry in the grandparenting numbers. Where was Nana's husband? they asked. The answers have evolved, from merely, "he died," (true, many years ago now) to, "he didn't live with us".

Unlike Justin Webb I don't feel the need to explain for their benefit about the grandfather they never had. To do so would seem akin to breathing life back into him. I have no desire to do that. One point Webb made did resonate though. He said his father was a presence in his life and a lack of presence all in one. Even though my absentee dad was not a television personality, I know what he means.

www.blogupnorth.wordpress.com

SAHDandProud

I'm a 39-year-old Stay-At-Home Dad (SAHD) with two amazing children under three. I'm not a writer, I'm not a journalist. I am a Dad and a Husband and I hope I'm doing well at both. Sometimes I don't think so. I'm no sainted figure and I'm never going to paint an inaccurate picture of what I am or what I can be. I can be grumpy. I love what I do. I have fun with my kids. Sometimes I hate what I do. Sometimes I feel lonely. My children's well-being is more important to me than my own. All in all, I'm a fairly normal parent. I'm told I'm not a normal person but I'm working on that one.

27 September 2011

The Interview

I've been thinking recently that when I attempt to return to some form of paid employment, when my daughter starts school in 2014, I would have been out of the workforce for five years. I've wondered if employers view stay-at-home parents who've been so for a considerable length of time as having been out of the work for so long that they're pretty much unemployable in comparison with people who have not been out of the workforce for so long, or if the skills you develop being a full-time parent are transferable to the world of the office. I was thinking about how the interview for my dream job could go.

Interviewer: Thanks for coming to see us, we just would like to speak to you in further detail about some aspects of your application, and would like you to give us some examples of the skills you said you possess.

Me: Fire away cocker, based on what I am about to tell you I'm a shoe-in for this job. *Leans back puts feet on desk*

Interviewer: You say in your application that you have excellent negotiation skills and you have applied these every day. Could you give me an example?

Me: I've successfully negotiated with my son, every day, since he was two on the subject of biscuits. He wanted a chocolate chip cookie every day. We negotiate, and when I present him with an alternative option, our friend, the banana, he usually accepts this. I have a 90% success rate, but I'm willing to undergo training to bring me to an acceptable level.

Interviewer: And an example of your excellent communication skills?

Me: Sure. Across a crowded playground I can successfully communicate to my son that he should not, and will not, try to run off with that girl's bike. I have excellent communication skills even at a volume that frightens horses.

Interviewer: Tell me more about your level of sickness and absenteeism?

Me: I haven't had a day off since 2009, working 12-14 hour days through sickness and illness. I've been know to get up at 5am and not finish until after 10pm. I'm pretty reliable.

Interviewer: Can you give me an example of a time when you've had a particularly difficult problem to solve and have solved it?

Me: Yes. My son didn't eat much fruit, but I invented the Hungry Caterpillar Week. On Mondays we had apple, and Tuesdays we had pears, Wednesday plums etc etc. He has now started to eat more fruit, but draws the line at strawberries.

Interviewer: You're an effective multi-tasker?

Me: I have been known to change both my son and daughter's nappies at the same time.

Interviewer: That's just one task you're doing twice though.

Me: Okay, I can cook three separate meals and do the hoovering while balancing a baby on one hip and a child on my head.

Interviewer: That's a better example. Thanks for that. And one last question. Could you tell me why you are the ideal candidate for this job?

Me: I'm cheap and I look good in a suit. I'm basically eye candy, but if you've been listening to my answers to the questions you've asked then I can tell you there are an estimated two and a half million stay-at-home parents who would be just as good at doing this job as me.

Interviewer: Well, thank you for applying for the job of Head of The Bank of England. We'll let you know shortly.

So, now I ask you, my friend, did I get the job?

www.sahdandproud.wordpress.com

Bringing up Charlie

Writer-in-residence at the mother-and-toddler group. Author of the best-selling parenting book for dads 'Fatherhood: The Essential Guide'

14 November 2011

Does being a stay-at-home dad make you less of a man?

This is a blog about a stay-at-home dad. One who has always felt fine in his own skin, not worried unduly about his identity, been ok with his own brand of masculinity. I've done this job – the stay-at-home dad bit – for three years now. But it's only recently I've thought seriously about this question thanks to an invite to discuss it on BBC Radio5Live.

Ok, I've been something of a curiosity at times. I was once invited to the local breastfeeding support group ('if you feel it would be useful') by a lovely lady who I think felt sorry for me – lone dad among a group of mums talking about something he couldn't really comment on. That was then, of course. Now, I can and do comment – and in writing. I've written an entire book on the subject (just in case anyone has missed it!) And I'm no longer 'lone dad'. I've made some good friends among the other mums; but there are also more dads around taking their kids to toddler groups. I'm no longer in a minority (locally) of one.

Of course, being something of a one-off can be advantageous and I can't say I haven't enjoyed some of the attention. But if I'm honest, I've always had this nagging feeling that – vital as it is, important as I know it to be and as enjoyable as I find being at home with the children – it wasn't, well, 'me'. At least, not all of me.

How we define ourselves is a complex issue and no doubt stay-at-home mums have known about this problem all along. But it's taken me some time to appreciate that the other part of my day-to-day existence – writing – is a useful cover. I can tell people that's what I do (a bit like Andrew Watson, the other guest on the programme) instead of own up to being nothing but a house husband. Because that does carry with it certain negative connotations – 'kept' man (I'd like to add 'toy boy' but age prevents me) and so on. The expectation is that I should be out there hunting, bringing home the bacon and then going to watch the football and having a beer. And this expectation isn't confined to men, either. So, with my sensitive antennae tuned to perfection, I pick up on the negative vibes and change my definition – of myself – according to the person I'm addressing.

Thus I'm sometimes Tim Atkinson, stay-at-home dad; sometimes Tim Atkinson, author; sometimes both. But why can't I simply be 'me'?

www.bringingupcharlie.co.uk

First-Time-Daddy

About the family. First up, the reason I go to work every day and the reason I started this blog: Baby Benjamin AKA 'BB'. Second up, our other little baby, man's supposedly best friend, the dog: Penny AKA 'Mentle'. Thirdly, the love of my life, who without, I wouldn't have my beautiful baby boy: Christine AKA 'The Mrs'. And last and definitely least, I'm Lewis AKA First-Time-Daddy.

17 October 2011

Becoming a dad isn't amazing.....

Let me explain. I recently went out for what some might call "Wetting the baby's head", whereas I just call it a few drinks with friends. We drank, laughed, we watched the mighty Leeds United beat local rivals Doncaster Rovers convincingly 3-0 and we drank some more. During one of the less random conversations that we had that night, one of my friends turned round to me and asked me "Does it feel amazing being a dad?" My initial response to this was "Yes, of course it's amazing." My friend knew how much becoming a dad meant to me and he knew that it had taken some years to convince the Mrs, so it wasn't a strange answer, but then I changed my mind. "It's not amazing really, it's..." and after a few seconds, he suggested "Natural?"

That was it! Becoming a dad wasn't an amazing feeling; it wasn't really any emotion other than it just felt right. It's weird how you imagine something being one way and when that's exactly the way it goes, the only feeling I have is one of content. So far, being a dad has been everything I could have hoped and dreamed of. BB is healthy, Christine has been more of an amazing mummy than I could have ever have imagined and BB is growing every day. When I see the littlest changes, the different kind of smile where you know this time, he is in fact laughing at you being silly and not just suffering from trapped wind. The first time he is laid playing and he squeaks with the first murmurings of a giggle, everything just feels... right. Even when he cries because he is hungry or the bad lady at the doctors keeps sticking needles in his legs, to sit there and comfort my boy until his tears stop falling, just feels... right.

As I type this it is 20:27 on 17/10/11, I realise that BB is exactly three months old (to the minute) and we have already seen such big changes in him. He recently started rubbing his eyes when he is tired, he has started sleeping through the night (about ten hours) and Christine is convinced that he is teething! (Not sure I believe that!) I look forward to seeing what else my little boy will learn to do in the next few months and next few years to come.

BB, happy three month birthday. Mummy and daddy love you very much.

www.first-time-daddy.blogspot.com

It's a Dad's Life

My name is David and I'm a new Dad. I started this blog as a way of expressing what I was going through as my wife and I neared the end of coupledom and entered the world of parenthood! I wanted to see what happened when my life became that of a Dad's. As well as putting my own thoughts down, I really wanted to create an honest record that other new parents may find helpful.

23 June 2011

I'd Stay Up All Night...

...just to make you happy. I think that sums up last night. Let me explain. Throughout the day I was getting text messages from my wife telling me how her day was going. Most of these messages contained something along the lines of "She's still awake!" or "She's so tired and grumpy but just won't sleep". That culminated in them meeting me at the station, in the rain, when I got home from work. "It really must be bad," I thought when I saw them there!

The evening progressed in much the same way. Due to the rather chaotic day, we decided to have Chinese takeout for dinner as a little pick me up, so once home we placed the order thinking she'd be asleep by the time it arrived. Silly us. A bottle of formula later she was still as grumpy as ever, rubbing her face but just refusing to settle. She was clean, fed, cuddled, not too warm, not too cold, nappy not too tight, clothes fitting well, room not too bright but nothing would settle her. So we left her to grumble in her cot while we tried to eat. That didn't really work either. It's hard to enjoy your dinner when your baby is crying her eyes out. But we needed to eat. A quick stuffing of satay later, I was back upstairs trying to figure out what she needed.

She guzzled another 90ml of formula – where she put it I have no idea but it seemed to settle her a little, but still not enough to allow her to slip off into sleepy bliss. What to try, what to try? Off came the shirt (mine) and then onto my chest she went. This seemed to settle her a little more, but again she was still refusing to sleep. After about 20 minutes of chest time I noticed her tummy was going hard, then soft, then hard, then soft. Aha! We've been here before. I know what that means. Someone is feeling a little bunged. So onto the bed we went, making circles with her legs and gently massaging her stomach. A few minutes later, all hell broke loose in her nappy. I imagine that's one of those rare occasions when you are ecstatic that your baby has done a poo. The effect was instant. The child lying on the bed had gone from a wriggling, grumpy person to someone who'd just had her switch turned off. She just lay there, legs out and arms flat behind her, staring into space. Woooo! Result! Oh no, wait, I need to change her now don't I? Damn.

A major cleanup operation (which really warranted the use of a HazMat suit) later she was back in her bed, this time slowly slipping off to sleep. Mum and I retired to bed to pass out. All were asleep by 10pm.

So what was the point of me telling you all that? Firstly, I suppose it might pop into your head when you're asking yourself "What's up with my baby?" at which point I hope you hear my voice saying "Poo blockage!" Mmmm. Secondly, it's just to say that, at no point was I not prepared to stay up all night with her, just to make her happy. My need for sleep was totally irrelevant.

I guess that's what being a dad is all about.

www.itsadadslife.co.uk

Dadsmidlifecrisis

Dear Reader and Confidante, I am a house husband primarily. Have been since the birth of our first child. I love my partner, and I love my children. I love this opportunity, to be the homemaker.

19 February 2010

Role Reversal

Heard yesterday from my osteo (whilst I was being crunched and popped) that he has a friend who is, like me, a stop at home dad; interestingly he is working on a book provisionally entitled 'We've been conned'.

Apparently its central theme is that women have for ages conned us into believing that the job of doing the domestic work and childcare is very, very, very difficult, and that we as men are not up to it.... and he thinks it is a breeze... grrrr!

I'd love to see his day/house/loft/fridge/playroom/laundry as I suspect that he is in denial as well as quite possibly at war with his wife. Or maybe has a team of manservants (woman-servants?) on hand and London's finest concierge service. I'd especially like to hear his wife's assessment of his performance. This seems to be a good example of that classic insecure over-achieving, over-ambitious 'can definitely do', 'deny every weakness' trait frequently exhibited by bottom-sniffing wannabe alpha males in corporate structures, such as the workplace he graciously resigned from to do the 'dadding'. It's 2010 – turn your gaze to the city and look where that thinking has brought us – so many of these men definitely could not do what they were either convinced they could or were told they could...

With more women at the helm would not the world be a slightly less greedy and bereft, but slightly more humane place right now? Whilst far from a perfect sex, women just have a better way of getting the job done from what I have seen. More harmony, soul, empathy, care, cooperation, foresight and forward motion; less bravado, less bullshit, less swagger, less dogma and definitely less misery. My own personal experience is that househusbandry has been the most challenging thing I have ever done, topping my youthful ambitions and efforts to become a rockstar (minor success but then it's a very competitive area!) and building two of my own businesses (slightly better efforts). I can see the odd grey hair, and my nerves are shattered from the baby-toddler lack of sleep thing. My tolerance is all used up. I will never be the same. I am uncertain of what talents I possess anymore.

So, I happen to think that if someone has found a way to do it effortlessly they should keep their bloody trap shut or write a book about it so we can all judge their methodology for ourselves… hence I will definitely be looking forward to the book he has planned hitting the shelves! Ok… back to the point I am trying to make, I think it's time for all men to respect the women in their lives more, trust and appreciate the unique talents of their partners in humanity – not belittle them with competitive alpha-male nonsense like this example. There is just a small chance that this way, the women they deal with may just respect and see more of the good in them, and then they'll no longer need to puff up their feathers in this insanely destructive way that takes us to war or to bankruptcy.

Men – don't be afraid; admit it – you're bored with behaving like you're in the playground! Open up and chill out a bit – find something to admit you're rubbish at, and get over your cocky selves! Somewhere between caveman and Metrosexual Moisturised Man there lies a happy path, where the woman you care about will still love you, want you and admire your unusual ways… and guess what? You're worth it!

www.dadsmidlifecrisis.blogspot.com

The Life and Times of a Househusband

I am a late 30s house-husband who finds it easier, and more amusing, to refer to himself as a housewife. I stay at home and bring up our three kids Dawn, Katy and Mate (as Katy calls him). My wife pretty much works full time in a fairly decent job, and I do a few part time bits and bobs that fit in around the kids. I have been a housewife for about 18 months now, and in my own humble opinion, I'm not doing a bad job. Which means I haven't broken one of them yet.

7 February 2011

The Electronic Nanny

This morning I found myself having an argument with someone about the Scooby Doo theme tune and how it had changed over the years. I'm a member of the old school and obviously prefer the classic quality of the original. My combatant sagely promoted the opinion that the arrangement of music in the new series 'Scooby Doo Mystery Incorporated' was far superior and catchy. They had a good point, but I'm not the greatest of losers, so I replied with a "Don't argue with your father, you watch too much TV."

I should really stop arguing with my five year old about kids' TV, her knowledge surpasses mine, and I guess that's partly my fault. I am quick to use the third parent, or 'the electronic nanny' as the faux posh refer to the television, whenever I need to get some work done. Hell, I use it if I want to get a moment's peace, and I need a lot of peace right now. I know traditional wisdom says that television should be used as a treat and that painting, drawing and reading should be the norm, and that opinion has value. Except that as a stay at home Dad I'm in a non traditional situation, so why can't I use painting and drawing as a treat, and the TV as the norm? Because my Mum said so, apparently.

On a recent visit my Mum asked Kaede what she had done today and to my shame, this was her reply. "Well first of all we watched Scooby Doo on Boomerang. Then we switched to CNToo so we could watch Johnny Test. After that Tom and Jerry came on, and it was Dad's favourite one, the one when all the balls hit Tom in the face. Then the Garfield Show came on but Dad thinks that sucks, so we turned over to Playhouse Disney, which is Nate's favourite, and watched Mickey Mouse then Little Einsteins." Apparently this is too much TV, apparently the kids need better stimulation, and apparently I am still scared of my Mum because half term started this week and I'm restricting the amount of TV being watched.

Day One didn't start too badly, we had a few tears and tantrums at first, but they soon calmed down. As the day wore on I did start to feel a little bit sorry for Nate. He was wandering around the house like he was being punished for something he couldn't quite remember doing. It was almost as if he was revisiting all his previous crime scenes and trying to figure out which one was to blame. Was it the crayon on the kitchen wall, the half eaten jelly bean in the carpet, or the scissors and his latest self inflicted Noel Gallagher haircut? The day passed without incident, and I will admit to being quite smug as I described our day to the Wife as we took the kids upstairs for bedtime. Smugness was soon running out of the house with his arse on fire when we saw the state of their bedrooms though. And the bathroom. And our bedroom. And all blue nail varnish on the hallway floor. And the same shade all over Nate's toes.

There was no TV for me that night, as I spent the evening on my hands and knees trying to get the blue footprints out of the carpet. I thought about drinking the nail varnish remover to cheer me up, it smelt so nice and inviting, but the room had started spinning already so I called it a night.

Day Two started with subdued children. I think the shock of watching their Dad trying to pull his own hair out the previous evening, may be the reason. Although the way they were intently watching the microwave as my reheated cup of coffee went round and round, made me think that they may be going cold turkey. Watching them put two chairs in front of the tank that housed our two bearded dragons, then sitting there for an hour watching them, convinced me. At least there were no adverts on that show though, which meant no shouts of "Can I have that, and that, oh and that", things were looking up.

I got them to do some drawing eventually, supplying a small copse worth of paper and a box of pens and pencils. Out of the 200 writing implements in the box, we managed to find seven that were either sharpened or full of ink, and Art 101 began. Kaede proudly showed me her first effort, a big black square with two sad faces next to it. Being a bit slow on the uptake, I asked her what the picture was. "It's the broken television with me and Nate sitting next to it crying" was her reply, accompanied by the saddest face she could pull. This convinced me of two things. Firstly, I was an awful parent. Secondly, women don't learn to become skilled manipulators, they are just born to it. For the rest of the day I could be found playing the role of referee in the world's longest wrestling match. The kids had been sent to, and sat in, so many corners of the house that I'm fairly sure they could draw accurate architectural plans of the place.

I don't normally drink on a Tuesday, well not publicly anyway, but that Tuesday my wife came home to a half empty (I used to be a half full person) bottle of Pinot Noir, and a not even starting to mellow husband. On Day Three I managed to write this piece. Yep, I caved. As I write, a bizarrely costumed villain has just uttered the immortal line "I would have gotten away with it too, it if wasn't for you meddling kids." The children are quiet other than the occasional shouted addition to their Christmas list, and all is good in the world.

www.goonerjamie.blogspot.com

Mutterings of a Fool

I'm a twenty something first time dad working for a large American corporation dreaming of a simpler life in the outdoors away from the office. This blog is a commentary on life as I see it, the ups and downs of raising a family and the challenge of using public transport every day to commute to work.

19 June 2011

Becoming dad

I'd been meaning to write this post for a while, but was finally motivated to do it when reading a post by Mother's Always Right. Firstly, this post is not intended to in any way to belittle how tough it is being a mum and what an amazing role mums perform, the lady of the manor is proof of that. But often I think it is overlooked how hard it can be for a new dad and I speak here from my personal perspective over the past nine weeks since Matilda was born.

It begins in the delivery suite, if you want a definition of a man feeling helpless it is this moment, you can be supportive and motivating all day but, ultimately, you have to sit back and watch in awe as your lady takes care of business so to speak. You are stripped of any opportunity to 'be a man' or demonstrate any of the qualities that we have evolved to have. You almost feel a little surplus to requirements.

Then you get home and the adrenaline and excitement wears off, leaving you with the sleep-deprived reality of the situation. Matilda was being breastfed so my role was tea boy, nappy changer and baby pacifier whenever she was crying. Fun times, although it was alright because I had all that paternity leave to get to know her right? Well those two days passed pretty quickly and then it was back to work (yes I know you can take two weeks on statutory pay, but who can afford to do that?)

Back to work and back to leaving the house at 7am five days a week and getting home at 6.30pm. The lady of the manor has done such a good job getting her settled in a routine, unfortunately that does mean that she's asleep when I get home. I get a cuddle at 11pm when I do a dream feed, but that's not really an opportunity to bond is it? I'm slowly becoming precisely the dad that I said I never would. One who doesn't know how to look after his children or know their routine and what they need. I want to be the dad that knows exactly how to cheer his little girl when she cries, who knows what her favourite food is and one that reads her a bedtime story every night.

On Thursday, I worked from home and realised what I'm missing, Matilda sat laughing and gurgling while the lady of the manor chatted to her. My little girl is changing every day and I hate the fact that she wouldn't smile for my like she did for the lady of the manor. So I need to change, I need to start spending time playing and interacting with her whenever I can. I need to forget the to-do list and jobs around the house and just relax, not something that I'm always very good at. A portion of the weekend needs to become dad time so we can have some quality time together. Today being father's day I did exactly that (after a small lie in of course), a fabulous cuddle on the sofa with my wee girl and the Brackster (who never passes up the opportunity for a cuddle).

Some other changes may be needed in the future if I'm going to be the dad that I really want to be, but for now this will do. My little girl smiles at me as I enter the room, what more can a man ask for?

www.mutteringsofafool.wordpress.com

Goodbye, Pert Breasts

I am the proud owner- I mean, father of a gorgeous boy, who has perfected the knack of making strangers go all gooey-eyed over him, whilst being a terror at home. My wife and I had another boy in April, and so I'm three on my way to a five-a-side football team. It was going to be 11-a-side, but the mrs would never allow it. For those who have asked, she has read everything that I've published on here, and is fine with it. Even if she wasn't, she'd never catch me.

29 August 2011

Are You Thinking What I Think You're Thinking?

The other day my 16-month-old son, Noah, was ever-so-slightly told off by my father-in-law for messing about with the TV remote control. His response – which I've never seen before – was to freeze, possum-like. For a good two or three minutes he just sat there, stock still, every now and then glancing at his granddad, who was looking as bemused as the rest of us. He even had his little chubby arm outstretched at the time: that, too, remained perfectly still.

Then, finally, he summoned the courage to crawl to me and burst into tears – which was good, because it meant I got a nice hug. But I also got to thinking about what must have gone through his head at the time; and this, I imagine, is how it went down.

Oh my word, what just happened?

Did he just tell me off? I think he just told me off.

What do I do? He's never told me off before.

When mum or dad tell me off I just ignore them,

but I don't feel I can do the same for this man.

He commands some kind of higher respect.

What do I do? Just sit still. Yeah, sit still.

Blend in with your surroundings.

You are carpet.

You are sofa.

They can't see you.

(Glances) Damn, it's not working!

They're all looking at me.

What do I do?

I've been very still for an awfully long time.

Oh boy, I think I'm going to cry.

Hold it together, Noah, it's not that bad.

It was only a sli- oh man, he's still looking at me!

What do I do? I have literally never been in this situation before.

You're going to crawl to dad.

Yeah, that's what you're going to do. Crawl to dad.

I can't move! I'm paralysed with fear!

Come on Noah, man up. You can do this.

They're all still looking at me. Now they're laughing!

I'm definitely going to cry.

OK, just crawl to dad, and it'll be fine. He gives nice hugs.

Do it. C'mon, DO IT!

After three.

One, two –

– oh hey, I can count! Didn't know that.

Focus! After three. One, two, THREE!

I'm crawling! I'm doing it! It's all too much! (Cries)

Hold me, father!

www.goodbyepertbreasts.com

Dad's in the kitchen

Howdy. I'm Tye Winston, a married father of four, finding my way through the wilderness of cooking, proof that an education, career and social life don't prepare a man for fixing dinners that kids will eat. It turns out, I'm not alone. So, I'm on a mission, to share survival tips, shortcuts, advice and occasional humor with men in the kitchen and the people who love them.

7 December 2010

Do Real Men Bake Christmas Cookies?

I was hanging lights from the peak of the roof the other day, and as I reached out for the farthest hook, trying to recall whether our insurance covered two-storey falls, a small crowd gathered in the yard near the ladder. This is somewhat of a holiday tradition. My wife sends the kids out to see if Dad's done a header, and the four of them stand shoulder to shoulder on the lawn and watch, ready to dash back in the house to report as soon as it happens.

Now, that's an invitation to joke. So, I swung one arm around my head, wobbled back and forth and made like I was losing my balance. Which, for one icy moment of electric fear, high on the extension ladder and one hand's reach too far from anything solid to grab onto, I did. The ladder screeched on the gutter, I leaned left, it stopped its slide and then it was over. Not the smartest thing I've ever done. And, sorry to say, scared the kids, proper. They hit the porch like the blitz and before I could get down to ground level had reappeared with their mother.

"What are you doing up there? The kids thought you were going to fall!"

"Just kidding around. All safe. How do they look?" I said, looking up.

"Not funny. Not one bit." She motioned with her eyes to the kids. The elder girls looked angry, the small kids still wide-eyed. Not going to let it go. I started to reassure them, but their mother steered me off. Now, my wife has a look. It's exactly the look I imagine she would have used if we were standing at the altar to get married, and I said, "Can I think about it?" when we got to the 'I do'.

"I have an idea," she said, and gave me that look. "Would you like to make cutout Christmas cookies with your Father?" she said. And to my surprise the frowns melted. Smiles came out. The neighbors came to the window to see who won the superbowl.

"Now…" I said, getting ready to explain why I'd be putting the chainsaw to some firewood rather than doing ballet with a rolling-pin and green frosting. But between the tugging and shouting, laughter and the look, I never got the chance. I don't know about you, but I remember my own mother, and grandmother, and cutout cookies at Christmas. Mostly, I remember how they rolled the dough just so, and carefully cut and then lifted the cookies onto baking pans ever so gently, so as not to break off heads or hands or tips of stars or trees in the process. And, I remember how they eventually gave in and just let me squash my broken attempts up into lumpy round Christmas balls. I became an expert at Christmas balls.

And I wasn't looking forward to making more as an adult. To make a long story short, I gave in. And, I was wrong. I ended up dusted in flour, with a real kitchen mess, a few dozen colorful cutout cookies and one pan burnt beyond eating, but four chirping, happy kids having the time of their life laughing at me and making cookies. We had a really good time. Holiday cheer. And they did some up specially, as gifts for Dad, to make up for my meager attempts.

After we put the kids to bed, my wife got busy with the pans and bowls.

"Now if you go and kill yourself, at least the kids will have one big happy Christmas memory to remember you by', she said. And threw me the dish towel to dry.

www.dadsinthekitchenblog.wordpress.com

Daddy Diaries

Dad to Alex and Elliot, husband to Emma. Writing about my experiences of fatherhood in a personal capacity. The views of the author are not always those of his wife.

17 June 2011

My father, who art in Basingstoke

It's nearly Father's Day. I'm cock-a-hoop about spending it with Emma and the boys. But it's also prompted me to write some things down about my own dad.

He's a man who has had a lot thrown at him in his time, but has never complained (at least not to me). He's loyal to the hilt – to my mum, and to me, his only child. He's a proud man. A funny man. He's not as well as he used to be, but through heart attacks, cancer and Parkinson's, he's rarely made a fuss.

He loves his dogs. He's devoted to his wife. He's a fighter. A grafter. He left school in his teens with no qualifications in the 1950s, worked bloody hard and once told me he wished he'd been around more when I was growing up. (I told him I'd never felt short changed). In his youth he worked as a builder's apprentice, a milk bar waiter, a window cleaner, a chauffeur and a car salesman. But above all, he's a salesman. An ideas man.

He's smarter than he makes out. He'd spend his last fiver on my mum and me (and at times, he probably has). He lives for the now and loves his grandsons completely. He tells my wife things he never told me. He's honest. Dignified. Generous in spirit and deed. I hope he's proud of me. He doesn't say 'I love you', but he doesn't need to. He has a scar on his leg where a rooster attacked him as a boy.

He's my dad and maybe one day I'll show him this. But I'll probably just send a card because nobody wants to see their dad cry.

www.daddydiariesblog.com

I've become my parents

This little blog has been growing and I am so grateful to have people reading I've Become My Parents. Your comments are awesome and you share some great stories with all of us. While I do blog anonymously, it seems a bit unfair that I get to call you by name (real or otherwise) and you all have to stumble around calling me things like, "Mr. My Parents" or "IBMP" or "You lousy, no good, sorry excuse for a parent". So I thought it would be a good idea to at least let you know who you're talking to and give you a name you can use when we're chatting here on the blog or when you're whining about me to your friends. My name is Barmy Rootstock. But you can call me Barmy. And I'll let you in on a little secret: that's not my real name. I know, right?

4 July 2011

Son, it's time we talked about sports

"Hey Dad, at the class picnic I was sitting there thinking everyone hated me and Danny came up to me and said I was 'hard to hate'. Isn't that a funny thing to say?"

The way you said that yesterday, son, totally caught me off guard. You said it as if the "everyone hated you" part was just some brief bit of context and the real point of the story was that Danny said something funny. That's like saying, "So I was crossing the street to get out of the way of these guys that just robbed a bank and the coolest looking car went by." Um, HELLO?

So I hope you'll understand if I stopped listening to the rest of the story after hearing that you were thinking that everyone hated you. I didn't think they still did that thing where kids all stand in a line and the two biggest jocks in the school get to pick who they want on their teams. I thought they stopped using the Line of Shame technique back when they did away with the dunce cap. Apparently I was wrong. It turns out that they were picking teams for volleyball – a game you've never played – and nobody wanted you on their team.

Why? Because they don't want to lose. That seems fair enough. Give a ten year old the choice and I'd expect they'd pick the kids most likely to help them win. OK, I get that but there are some things you need to know: First of all, you can't suck at something you've never tried. The suckometer can't even detect suckiness until you've at least tried something first. Saying you suck at volleyball is like me saying I suck at brain surgery. I'm actually not a bad surgeon – because I'M NOT A SURGEON. And, besides, not picking you isn't the same as hating you even though it usually feels like it is. But you know what concerns me most? It's that you were totally resigned to the idea that you just aren't good at sports. At the age of 10 you've decided that you just aren't a "sports guy".

So here's my little dadfable for the day:

One upon a time in a land remarkably similar to where I grew up, there was this kid. We'll call him... me. This kid we're calling me joined Little League because some friends did. Now, it turns out that, for a lot of dads, the size of their penis is demonstrated by how well their kids do in sports. So most of the other dads had taken two weeks off work to run their Li'l Sluggers through an intensive Baseball Training Home Bootcamp. I guess the idea was to ensure that their kids had already mastered how to play baseball before joining the program that's supposed to teach them how to play baseball. In this way, the dads would ensure that their penis size was duly noted and they wouldn't have to buy a Hummer.

My pre-training training, on the other hand, consisted of stopping at Wal-Mart on the way to the first practice to buy a glove. And you know what's awesome? It took a bunch of tries, but I actually hit the ball on the first day of practice! With the bat, even! I made it to second base, which is pretty cool in either of its connotations (we'll talk about that some other time). I was feeling pretty good; with some practice, I could probably do this baseball thing. Now, I knew enough about baseball to understand that the idea is to run from base to base and then get back to home plate. So when the next guy hit a high fly ball, I bolted for third feeling pretty damn good about myself while the other kids cheered me on yelling, "Tag up, tag up." Assuming that was some kind of cry of encouragement, I kept running, rounded third and made it across home plate, pumping my fists in victory.

So I was rather confused when my teammates told me I was out and had ruined their day, and quite possibly the rest of their lives. It turns out that, if the other

team catches a fly ball and you're not standing on a base, you're out. Any idiot that attended their dad's pre-season baseball bootcamp would have known

that tagging up means to keep a foot on the base and wait to run until you see whether they catch the ball. The rest of the team treated me like the lamo they thought I was for the rest of the season. And the problem is so did I. I had plenty of time to ponder that while I picked dandelions in left field. I didn't touch another bat after that rather painful season was over. And for the most part, I avoided just about all other team sports. I just wasn't a "sports guy".

I'm no Aesop, but there's a moral in there somewhere, and it has nothing to do with penis size (well, maybe a little). The bottom line is that you don't suck at sports, and neither did I. But I did suck at trying new sports for a very long time after that. And trying new sports is worth practicing. So how about we go hit some balls?

www.ivebecomemyparents.com

Fatherhood[2]

A collection of musings, thoughts and brain-emissions, mainly on the topic of Fatherhood.

19 October 2011

Routine – The Joys and the Sorrows

I don't profess to be anywhere near an expert in parenting – in fact, I'd go as far as to say that in a lot of respects I'm nothing more than an amateur. But what I DO know is what has worked (and not worked) for my children. Routine is one thing that has made our lives a LOT easier – and occasionally a little trickier…

The Joy of Routine

As a parent, routine is your friend. Routine can make your life a lot easier. Little children LOVE routine – they gobble it up, and it gives structure and sense to their chaotic little lives. Take bedtime for instance. Before I became a parent, I would regularly scoff when I heard about parents who would stick laboriously to routines for their children. "Look at them, missing out on a beer because they HAVE to give little Timmy a bath at a certain time – what FOOLS!" I would say. But now that I'm a father of two, I recognise how foolish I was. Having a bedtime routine is joyous.

Our current bedtime routine for Robert (and soon for Freddie too) consists roughly of: Dinner, 30 minutes of "wind down" time with CBeebies, a bath, two stories and in to bed. It has been this way since he was about six months old (from the moment where he could happily sit still for a story, basically) and the consistency of this routine almost guarantees he will go to sleep within about five minutes of jumping in to bed. No matter how chaotic or different your day – even on holiday – keeping to this routine has always worked a treat for us, at a time that some parents can find an absolute nightmare.

On a smaller scale, routine can help with more day-to-day tasks: Always washing your hands after you've had a wee, put your toys away once the day is done, holding hands before you cross the road. I wouldn't say we've cracked all of these to the same level as bedtime, but they certainly take advantage of your child's burgeoning memory.

But at the same time as being a key weapon in your parenting arsenal, routine can also blow up in your face – though recognising this is happening can be half the battle…

The Sorrow of Routine

Take the bedtime example above. If we stick to this routine, everyone's a winner. Minor changes here and there can easily be glossed over, but make a more significant change (particularly one which is construed as positive to the child) and you can kiss your little routine goodbye. For instance, bedtime stories: Occasionally, I would offer Robert a third story as a "reward" for something. Short-term gain – long-term pain. For the next three plus nights, he'll demand three books, and the ensuing fall-out will dramatically disrupt bedtime, sometimes to the extent that he'd end up with no stories at all. Not a happy bunny!

You can also find yourself in unintentional routines too. I don't know if you took part, but last week The Sun newspaper (not something I'd usually buy, I should add) were doing an offer where you got a free LEGO model with every copy, for a week. For four days in a row (I missed a few!) I was able to get two Lego models for just 60p, so Robert and I were able to sit down together during breakfast and make our models (he's surprisingly good at LEGO for a three year old!).

All very nice and heart-warming, until the day when the promotion came to an end. Even now, six days later, he still asks me excitedly in the morning whether we'll be "building our models" over breakfast – with the ensuing micro-tantrum throwing a spanner in the works of our morning routine several times. So routines can be a pain, too – especially when you didn't realise you were establishing them.

I'm sure there are lots of other examples, but you get the picture. Overall I'd say the "Joy" of routine wins out over the "Sorrow" – even getting the hang of recognising a routine will help you in combating (or exploiting) them…

www.henrysblog.co.uk

Military Dad

I'm in the military. I'm a dad. I blog. Awesomeness ensues.

7 May 2011

How did I become a fake swearer?

I always used to laugh at the people that would stub their toe and then exclaim, "Fudge!" Come on, people, just let the real swear words fly. You'll feel much better about it. It's like a weight has been lifted off your chest, and your pain just magically disappears. Behold the power of cursing!

When I was young, I would sit on the floor with my father and listen to George Carlin records where I learned pearls like "the seven words that you can't say on TV." I took pride in my ability to tie together impressive strings of expletives. I am a sailor, after all. I have a reputation to uphold and stereotypes to live up to. I could make firefighters run for cover. Grown men would curl up in the foetal position with a feeling of awe, and young boys would make a bee-line for the nearest church. Young girls would hide behind their mothers' skirts, who would in turn hide behind their mothers' skirts and so on, until there were several generations of women hiding behind each other. Let's just say that I could make an impact. Then I had kids and things changed.

I don't think there were any exact moments where I decided that I couldn't carry on with my old ways, but it probably started around the time my daughter turned 18 months old and started repeating everything I said. What used to be a great tool for motivating and entertaining my sailors instantly turned into a potential dinner party nightmare. All of a sudden, fake swearing started to hold some appeal. I started out slowly just to see how it would feel. I'd toss out a "darn," "dang," or "frick" every once in a while. I didn't get laughed at or burst into flames, so I started to wade in a little deeper. If I spilled my coffee, I'd shout "crap sticks" for all the world to hear. Hitting my thumb with a hammer would bring out a nice "mother of mercy!"

As I got more comfortable, I realised that fake swearing can be fun. If something perplexes me, I ask, "what the deuce?" (stolen from Family Guy). If something surprises me, I'll unleash my personal favourite (and the one that gets the most chuckles) "Sweet Baby Buddha!!!"

It's been a long and eventful journey from master of the four-letter word to purveyor of the tame phrases. It hasn't always been smooth, and there have been mistakes along the way. My daughter has certainly blurted out a word or two that would make oil-rig roughnecks blush, but for the most part, I've been able to control myself. It's been rewarding, and if I've caught an odd look a time or two, it's worth it. While I still have all of those George Carlin records, I probably won't sit on the floor and listen to them with my kids (it helps that I don't actually have a record player anymore). I'm still not perfect, by golly, but at least my kids won't get me thrown out of any restaurants in the near future.

www.militarydadblog.com

Chronicles of a Reluctant Housedad

In July last year, my wife and I swapped roles after I was made redundant. I made hundreds of attempts to find another job as a manager but failed, so my wife gave up being a full-time mum and went out to work. I started writing my blog as a chronicle of life-change and how I cope with being a very reluctant housedad to my nine-year-old stepdaughter and our two sons, aged six and three, and how my Successful Other Half copes with the fallout.

7 May 2011

Men think about food more than sex, says a report. But is it true?

A report in the newspaper this morning says that the notion of men thinking about sex, sex, sex, on the minute, every minute, every day, no matter what their age or physical condition, is a myth. What we actually think about, says the report, is food and sleep. Is this true? For the past couple of hours, I've been keeping a diary of my thoughts to see how often sex enters them. Here are the results of my scientific study:

7.45am: Location: Bed, with wife

Thoughts: 'Is that the time? The kids aren't up yet. Why not? Something must be wrong. Who cares? Another hour's sleep. Yippee!'

7.55am: Bed, with wife

'Bloody hell, the kids ARE up. It can't be my turn again. It's ALWAYS my turn. But look at my lovely sleeping wife, all serene and beautiful in her nakedness. Should I, eh? Should I? Should I wake her up and tell her THEY'RE HER BLOODY KIDS, TOO, SO WHY DOESN'T SHE GO DOWNSTAIRS AND MAKE THEM BREAKFAST?'

8.15am: Kitchen, with kids

'God, I'm knackered. Shouldn't have had that second bottle of red last night. Oooh, but that steak was nice. Nothing like a juicy Friday night steak. Wish I'd saved some. I'd slice it up and put it on a sandwich with some mustard. Actually, I'm starving. Where's the bacon? What? We've no friggin' bacon? Jee-suss Ker-ist, who forgot to get the friggin' bacon? Oh, it's me. Shite. I'll have to settle for a few dry Cheerios for now.'

8.45am: Bedroom, with wife

'I know she's had a hard week and I know she'd love a cuddle, but I'm half-dressed now. The shops will be open soon. Sausage, bacon and mushrooms, yeah that would work.'

9.01am: Shop

'Decisions, decisions. Choices, choices. Er, not 99% pork sausages – the skins are too thick and chewy: just doesn't work on a sandwich. Bacon? Wiltshire Dry Cure, that's a given. And flat field mushrooms. Very meaty. Can't beat 'em.'

9.20am: Bedroom

'She's got that look in her eye. Ignore it. Ask her if she wants melted cheese on her sandwich. She doesn't. That's fine by me. I could get all this done and dusted in 20 minutes – plenty of time for Saturday Kitchen.'

9.40am: Kitchen

'Hope it rains. If it rains, I don't have to take the kids to the park. Is it too early for them to play on the computer? It can't do any harm, can it? Half an hour, tops. Just 'til I've eaten this. Yep, then we'll go out.'

9.50am, Bedroom, with wife

'Oh my word, that was lovely. The sausages were caramelised just so; the bacon was perfectly crisp; and the mushrooms just took the whole sandwich to a different level.'

9.55am: Bedroom, with wife

'Five minutes 'til Saturday Kitchen. Mmm, she does look pretty lovely, my missus. I wonder if, y'know, if I chanced my arm, she might be, y'know, be interested…? Shag, Saturday Kitchen, sleep! I mean, it's got to be worth a try. He who dares wins, Rodney, and all that.'

10am: Bedroom, alone

'Ah well, James Martin's not a bad second choice. Ooh, and Christ Tarrant's 'Food Heaven' choice could be a winner. Slow-roast shoulder of lamb. Mmm, lovely. Hey, that's a thought, what are we going to have for dinner tonight?'

www.reluctanthousedad.com

Comfort in Sound

I'm 26 (nearly 27) years of age, with a love of football and cricket. I recently became a father and enjoy life, never try to stress out over anything except three points on a Saturday. Fitness is the game I work in and I love my job, as well as my family, and Neighbours (the TV show).

16 November 2011

T minus 3 days and counting......

So it's finally here, we are within our last week of pregnancy (hopefully) three days to be precise until the baby, our new addition to our little family is due. I'm sure many fathers can relate to this post. By what I am about to write I hope I don't sound like I'm whinging, quite the opposite, I can't wait to be a father and understand my girlfriend has had to deal with so much and love her deeply so for going through it all.

This week, this time is very scary, and horrible but as equally, weirdly, exciting. You may notice the words there, let's break them down. Firstly scary, why is this time scary? Well any day now, I will be a father for the first time. I am solely responsible, as well with my partner for the health and wellbeing of another. This child will look up to me need me to care for it, feed it, bathe it, clothe it, all round be responsible for it. This can be quite a scary though, couple that that the first couple years of the child's life it can't actually tell me what is wrong. I've looked after and worked with children before but they have always been able to communicate with me verbally, telling me when they needed feeding, when they weren't feeling well. For these reasons alone this time is scary as the ticking clock draws nearer.

However it is also scary to know that soon enough my girlfriend will be screaming all sorts of obscenities towards me accusing me of doing all this to her, and then knowing that in some way she will be plotting her revenge.

Ok so the next word, Horrible. Why is this time horrible? For this sole reason, and I hope other dads felt like this. Picture the scene, you're sitting comfortably on the couch with your heavily pregnant loved one. She then winces in pain, you jump up saying are you ok? Is it contractions? Shall I get the car ready? Already halfway out the door with your jacket on clutching the hospital bag that resembles something more like you used when you went backpacking for six months, than a simple bag to take to the hospital. Your girlfriend then smiles and goes "no, I just had a pain in my big toe". At this point the man wants to say, "I don't care about your big toe, I thought you were going into labour!" This time is also horrible as every time you are not with your partner and your phone starts ringing you are again, halfway out the door with your coat on just to realise the person on the other end of the phone is someone trying to sell you a credit card or something, and you have to muster all your strength to politely tell them where to go.

Lastly exciting. Well this needs no real explanation. It is such an exciting time to know that, any day soon, our baby who my girlfriend has carefully looked after and loved and had to carry around for the last nine months will be here ready to meet everyone, meet her eagerly-waiting big sister and her Nanny, Nana and Grandpas and, most importantly in my eyes meet me. My girlfriend has had nine months getting to know the baby and feels this fantastic connection and even though I often speak to the baby and feel its twists it turns and its kicks and punches, I will feel an even deeper connection when I get to hold my child in my arms for the first time and see their little face; this will make all the times I've jumped towards the car and revenge my girlfriend will throw at me all worthwhile.

But then you think, "I've passed my DNA on to an unsuspecting world, what have I done?"

www.comfortinsounds.blogspot.com

Daddacool

I'm Alex, the daddy to two wee nippers. M'laddo is four and the lass who has just turned two but has the lungs of a fully grown opera singer. I'm married to wifey, who writes beingamummy.co.uk. I'm normally a bit rubbish at blogging but since my entire office gets massive doses of what the little 'uns get up to, I thought it was time to blog. Seems only fair.

22 July 2011

Ninja Kids and the Gonad Assault

In what must be a first, I'm blogging about my balls. They hurt (again) and not because of anything pleasant. Since he was tall enough to walk and strong enough to swing a punch, the boy has been almost demented in his desire to punch me in the balls. Perhaps it's his way of telling us he wanted to be an only child. If it is, Fifi is evidence his approach failed and philosophically perhaps he should have considered some sort of drawing or painting instead.

The most memorable ball whack came on our visit to the Chiltern Open Air Museum. It was a cool and overcast day and since we arrived there at opening time, due to a typical Fifi early start, we were the first and pretty much the only visitors in there when we were hailed by the head of the friends association. I only got as far as putting my hand out to shake his because at that point, the boy stepped out smartly from behind me, punched me hard in the balls and vanished. His vanishing wasn't exactly of Houdini standards mind, since somewhat involuntarily I decided to double up and writhe on the floor in agony. Goodness only knows what the head of the friends association thought about it all. Perhaps he was just glad his balls were unmolested.

It happened twice today too, which was both baffling, painful and sad too. We've had a great day today, paddling in the sea, running up and down the beach, digging holes, putting 2ps in 2p machines at the amusement arcade and sitting on the front eating fish and chips. Most kids would show their thanks with a cuddle or a thank you. Mine showed his love by punching me in the balls. This was a feat he repeated whilst getting ready for bed, which was all the more baffling as he was in the process of telling his Uncle about all the coins he'd saved from the clutches of the 2p machine.

So now I have aching balls again and a sense of frustration* because it's not something that the boy does all the time, or even a lot of the time but he does it often enough that it's blooming irritating. I've tried all sorts of approaches to stop him doing it and he does seem genuinely sorry afterwards, he just won't stop punching me in the balls.

*and not the usual sort of frustration involving their balls that blokes get either

www.daddacool.co.uk

Confessions of a real stay at home dad

I am me. I am golden. Gorgeous. Romantic. Sensual, caring, creative; But (and I believe I am perfectly entitled to feel like this....) I am also one very upset, unloved and neglected, sad, lonely, angry, sexually frustrated 'ex rock star stop-at-home dad'. Midlife crisis?

14 November 2010

Vom bug

Jeez we've all lost a stone in three days.

Seems there's a new winter vomiting bug that takes out your knees via inner ear (and thus balance) nerve infection, then as a real treat, it gets to work on your gut.

A real nasty; I won't be posting any pics... 'on the plus side' (there is ALWAYS a silver lining)... I have had two lovely days with boyo at home and we've been cuddled up on the sofa together watching every known episode of Shaun the Sheep, Sarah Jane Adventures and even, for posterity's sake, some old Numberjacks. Most of the teachers were off with it anyway... so no big loss of educational progress?

He's been inseparable from me but then talking to God on the big white telephone is a new one for him (since his forgotten babyhood experiences) so he's been a little freaked. Love him, he's a trooper. Will really miss him this week (though I still have his bug to keep me company).

Soooo... Night, night; it's finally bath time for stinky Daddy.

www.stopathomedad.blogspot.com

DaddyNatal

I'm Dean Beaumont the only fully qualified male Antenatal Educator in the UK. DaddyNatal is not my job, it's my passion. I now pioneer a range of services, products and support targeted for men and empowers them to become the parents which they want to be. I trained for the Diploma of Childbirth Education (Dip CBEd) through Childbirth International.

25 March 2011

Two Under Two

I'd like to introduce you to my children and discuss what it's like to have two children so close in age. My little boy, O, is now two years, nine months and my little girl, W, is one year eight months. There is almost exactly 13 months between them in age. We could have had two under one if we had really tried!

We always wanted to have our children close in age; to be truthful, we were aiming for more of an 18 month age gap… but that myth about being most fertile after just giving birth proved to be true for us and it was a case of almost first time lucky! Lots of opinions abounded when we announced our second pregnancy, including the fact we must be certifiably mad! However, we believed there would be benefits to having them so close together. Particularly that having them close together in age would reduce the sibling rivalry and jealousy that can occur.

Just to make life interesting, following our experiences from O's birth, both Steph and I had decided to train to work with expectant and new parents. On top of this, we were starting our own business, parents to a baby under one, pregnant with baby number two and I was still in full-time employment!! Hmmm, put like that, maybe the certifiably mad comment wasn't too far of mark!

What was noticeable, once W was born and especially in those first weeks and months, was the total love for W had for her brother and vice versa. At no point did O appear, or act, as if he resented her or needed to compete for attention. He has, from the first, always looked out for W, always looked to get her things and in the early days was willing to share everything with her… (that bit is starting to wear off now though!) Of course, with every upside comes the natural downside. For Steph, the sheer work involved in looking after a newborn and a 13 month old was certainly taxing to say the least, let alone the rest on her plate. However, the initial bond that developed between the two of them was immensely strong and continues to be so. I sincerely hope it always will be.

For me, the sheer joy of seeing them enjoy each others' company and interact with each other is immeasurable, it is one of those heart-melting moments you get to enjoy as a parent.

The thing I find both amazing and worrying at the same time, is the way they mimic each other. This has happened since the very early days and it is, without doubt, for me, a double-edged sword. On one hand, W through mimicking O, has developed an amazing vocabulary for one so young. Her speech is so far ahead of where O was at this age. However, on the other hand, I do have moments of concern that O mimicking W causes him to regress in some ways. O never really took to comforters, apart from a spell when he was quite young, after that he would suck his thumb to comfort himself when going to sleep, but that was about it. W, on the other hand has always been a hand sucker, (yes, her whole hand generally) and this is something that, in recent months, O has now taken to as well.

Overall though, they both benefit as they can constantly interact with each other and have developed excellent social skills for children so young. This interaction includes some basic sign language we have taught them, and some O has learned from another little boy, during his one day a week in nursery. W has already turned the tables on her big brother and is now, without doubt, the boss of this relationship. While it used to be O who would be able to pin W to the ground during a wrestling match, now W wins those matches every time!

O is incredibly kind-hearted, and will do almost anything for his sister, which has certainly helped us on a number of occasions. O loves playing with his little sister, and now the first thing he wants to do when he wakes up in the morning is go and see her. Even if it does mean no lay in for us! Oh, for a lay in! This has now progressed to the second he wakes, jumping out of bed, running down the hall, opening her door and vaulting over the side bars of her cot to actually get in and see her.

Bath time is now excellent fun (well for three of us, not so sure Steph enjoys it!) I have always encouraged much splashing in the bath to make sure the kids have no fear of water on their faces. O used to take great delight in splashing himself, mummy, daddy and W. Here again though, W has turned the tables and really, really goes for it with her splashes, soaking everything and everyone in the bathroom. The common cry now is from O shouting 'stooooooooooooooppp!' That said, we have two totally fearless children, who I have no doubt will cause Steph many missed heart beats and sleepless nights! Steph keeps trying to dress W in girly clothes, but I have a feeling she will be quite a tomboy in years to come (result for daddy!) They are definitely now at the age when they can be thrown, dropped and generally flung around and will ask for more!

According to the experts, a child really doesn't play with another child until they are at least two years of age. Really? Must introduce them to ours, because they definitely enjoy playing together and have done for a long while. O is the more laid back of the two and W will normally win any argument. That said, it has become noticeable that this is wearing thin and O is fighting back and not so willing to concede. We are really starting to see their individual personalities appear which is amazing and makes each day special. I could go on forever, but will include updates on the children from time to time. Suffice to say, I love my children and Steph dearly and I wouldn't change a thing. I still believe our instincts and choices, to have them close together was the right one, and although it is difficult at times (more so for Steph than me, as I get to go to work) I honestly wouldn't change a thing.

www.daddynatal.co.uk

Musodad

Music/Dad Blog crossover. I once told someone that "music is the universal love" over and over again on a night out. They haven't spoken to me since.

4 November 2011

Nick Cave and The Bad Parents – what not to do in the Peak District with two young children

WORLD EXCLUSIVE – "musodad in blogging about something other than music shocker!" You can see the front pages of the newspapers tomorrow already, can't you?! (Or maybe page 54, hidden within the classified section).

So why the change in direction? Well, in true music industry style, sometimes you need to diversify or get left behind. As much as I love them, if Oasis ("oh bloody hell – I didn't think he was going to talk about music!") had experimented a bit more, they might still be around today. It's good to keep things fresh and keep on moving – a bit like The Littlest Hobo.

So anyway, here is my first non-music related blog post (*takes deep breath*), which incidentally has a few music references in it anyway! Last Friday, my wife and I took our kids (aged four and 11 months) down a cave in the Peak District. You've probably guessed by now that the cave wasn't called 'Nick', it was in fact called 'Speedwell'. 'The Bad Parents' are my wife and I.

My wife and I had been down a couple of the caves there on previous visits (pre-kids) but had never experienced Speedwell – the one with the boat – as the queues are usually massive. Today though we were in luck – we were first in the queue! Just before we went in, spirits were high and we were beaming at the thought of 'going underground' (by The Jam). O was a little scared but our excitement soon rubbed off on her.

An hour later, on breathing the fresh Derbyshire air again, our thoughts had turned from 'this is going to be brilliant' to 'what the hell were we thinking?!' Now, I don't know if you've been down Speedwell Cavern, but when you first go in you have to descend 106 steps – 'easy peasy' we thought. However, when the ceiling is as low as it was, it's bloody difficult to negotiate with two kids! While I held O's hand, my wife carried C. All the adults were given hard hats but the kids weren't and poor C. had no protection from the unlevel, sharp rock sticking out of the ceiling (Bad Parenting example 1).

Once we had descended the stairs we came to the boat – it held about 20 people. We were still in a positive mood at this point, looking forward to seeing some cavernous, erm... caverns with stalactites of all shapes and sizes. Just to let you know – these were a bit rubbish! The tour guide sat at the front of the boat and literally had to push us down the river using the cave ceiling and walls to help the boat along. Again there was a lot of head ducking to be done.

At this point C was getting restless so we plied her with rice cakes, and then a rice cake dropped on the floor of the boat – noooooooooooooooooooooooooooo! Then, she wanted to stand up but she wasn't wearing shoes (Bad Parenting example 2) so her socks got all soggy! It was horrendous – and there was no escape! The tour guide then told us the boat trip would last about an hour – noooooooooooooooooooooooo! (again).

Eventually, after about 20 minutes, we made it to the other end of the river where we got out and the people who were already there stole our boat and we had to wait for the next one. As the boat was a bit wobbly on disembarking, I handed O to the tour guide and he put her down on safe ground. I then handed him C and he tried to stand her up without support on unlevel cavernous ground! (Bad Parenting example 3 – don't ever hand your 11 month old to a tour guide with no kids!) Luckily I got there just in time to catch her! Anyway, we stayed at the 'not as impressive as other caverns I have visited' cavernous bit for another 20 minutes, were shown about six really tiny stalactites and a flat (!) stalagmite – and then it was time to get back in the boat and go back. And for some reason (the tour guide did explain why but I can't remember cause my head was so numb!) it was bloody freezing on the way back!

We made it back to the stairs eventually and then had to walk back up them all until we finally made it back to street level and breathed a sigh of relief. FREEDOM!!!!!!!

Would I recommend it? Of course – it's an experience you're not going to get in many places, just please leave any kids under the age of four in the world above (accompanied by someone, of course). So there you have it, my first non-music related post. Hope you enjoyed it. If you think I should stick to music, then please don't hesitate to let me know.

www.musodad.blogspot.com

Files and Records

Father of five, husband to a wonderful wife, cook, geek. IT technician for a chunk of the UHI. Currently residing on a cold and windy rock around 60 degrees north off the coast of Scotland.

4 August 2011

How to have a holiday with five kids

Plan everything

As I said on Twitter recently, with five kids you can't do spontaneous. You can make things appear to be spontaneous but there's a lot of planning involved. Out recent holiday involved staying with friends and relatives in four different places across the country and at the Davy Crockett Ranch near Disneyland Paris. I'll say it again, five kids. That's seven people dropping in to visit, and if you're spending the night that's a lot of spare beds. Sometimes I envy those of you with only one or two kids; you can almost drop in unannounced. Right up until the morning before we were due to head to one of our overnight stops we had a backup plan in place!

Involve the kids

Where possible. Obviously don't try and get a two year old involved in planning the route you're going to drive, but my older kids found it great fun to get the map out and see where we were going to be and have some say into what we were doing. Get t'internet out and have a look around the area you're going to be in, see what sort of things there are to do that will entertain all ages. If one of yours has a particular interest or preference, try and work it into the plan. Not only will involving the kids make them feel better about the holiday, it will ramp up their excitement!

Picture the scene. We're in the kitchen, the younger kids are in bed, we unfold the map of Disneyland Paris. We've the Unofficial Guide to Disneyland Paris (a worthwhile investment if you're going that way) open and the computer ready to look stuff up. We spent a very happy couple of hours with our eldest planning which rides to do and when, checking out the reviews in the book, watching the videos on YouTube. Of course, we rewrote the plan several times…

Indoors if wet

Helmuth von Moltke the Elder once said "No plan survives first contact with the enemy." This can be revised to "No holiday plan survives first contact with the weather." Always have a backup plan for that sinking moment when you open the curtains and see wall-to-wall rain. No child enjoys being dragged around Roman ruins, no matter how impressive, if it's raining. For every day that involved activities outside, we had a backup day that was almost entirely indoors.

F'rexample. Vikings. We do a lot of stuff with Vikings on Shetland, not all of it particularly historically accurate, but a lot of it nonetheless. So this holiday we resolved to do no Viking stuff at all. I know Jorvik has been upgraded since my last visit and I'm dying to see what they've done now, but this holiday started off with Romans. Corbridge, where we started our trip, is near Hadrian's Wall, and within a half-hour drive are two of the most amazing Roman sites – Vindolanda (Yes, the one from Gladiator – "I fought with you at Vindolanda") and its sister exhibit, the Roman Army Museum. Vindolanda alone is worth the entry fee – it's where the wooden tablets were discovered giving us the most detailed insight into Roman life in Britain – and you can get entry to the Roman Army Museum for a few pennies more. Throw in some Gift Aid and you're virtuous and golden.

Point is, Vindolanda is mostly outdoors and the Roman Army Museum is indoors. So when we woke up to rain, we headed for the museum and did Vindolanda the next day when it was dry. If it hadn't been dry the next day, there was a massive swimming pool complex in Newcastle that was #1 on the agenda. Further south in Ripon, the outdoors plan was the Forbidden Corner, indoors the Royal Armouries in Leeds. It was raining, we hit the Armouries.

With Disneyland Paris it was a little trickier. Our plan for there if wet was to have coats and brollies within reach. Much of the queuing is under cover but getting from one ride to the next could've been very wet indeed. We were lucky given the rain we'd had in England and the rain Paris had been having!

Exit strategy

If you've got your attraction right, the kids won't want to leave. You need an exit strategy to make sure they're not wailing and howling all the way back to the car. I find the promise of ice cream is a good one. Or the Next Big Thing. "Oh, you think this place was great, just wait until you see…" Failing that, there's always the playparks. Hexham has a particularly good one my kids know and love.

Meals

If your family has a routine when it comes to mealtimes, it's not a good idea to try and break this one on holiday. The kids feel happy to have the comfort of the routine even if they're in a strange place. It helps to settle them. If you're going to be somewhere around lunchtime, check out the lunch opportunities. Cafes, pubs, etc. And if you think "Oh, that looks like a good pub" but it's got three coaches in the car park, move on. Pushing things past established mealtimes leads to fractious kids, stressed parents and bad decisions.

Diaries

It's been a tradition of our family, since my wife and I first got together and went to Zimbabwe back in the 1990s, to keep a holiday diary. We record everything – what we did, saw, ate, drank, how we felt. Every now and then we go to the bookshelves and pick up one of these volumes, dive back into our time in Zim, or Canada, Estonia or Egypt. Even if the holiday takes us only as far as England, if we're going away we keep a diary. We're encouraging our kids to do this too – if nothing else it keeps them practicing their handwriting during the school holidays!

For the kids, there's the added bonus of already having a pre-written answer to the inevitable "What did you do in your holidays?" question they'll get asked when they return to school. If they've added in photographs, entry tickets and brochures to the places they've visited so much the better. One thing I find particularly hard on holidays is knowing what day of the week it is. Having this written large across the top of each entry helps immeasurably!

Souvenirs

I find this one tricky. I know what I want the kids to take home from the gift shops; it's just that what they want is something completely different. Set a budget, offer advice and guidance, and be prepared to walk away with nothing. I have my Holiday Hat – a floppy green fishing hat I picked up in Lanzarote that the kids find embarrassing – and whenever I visit somewhere I get a pin badge for my hat. Disneyland was a revelation with the sheer range of pins available! I could've spent a large fortune collecting them all. Chances are that whatever the kids choose will be lost or broken before the holiday's done. Don't sweat it. They'll have plenty of chances to go back in later life, hopefully with their own kids, and realise that you were right about what they should have bought.

Photos

Looking back on this last holiday, I was surprised at how few photos I took. I was too busy having fun and spending time away from work with my kids.

Final words…

Fail to plan = Plan to fail. Trite, I know, but true. In the Internet Age it's inexcusable to turn up at a theme park and not know where the good rides are, what your strategy for getting to them quickly is, where the nearest toilets are and so on. An hour spent working stuff out before you go can turn a day from disastrous, aimless wandering to triumphant success.

www.blog.filesandrecords.com

The iDad

Parenting: the unconventional way

6 June 2011

Beware of the Growling Baby

"This is normal, this is normal... it must be normal?!" The words that I repeated over and over to myself after I had spent a day witnessing my six-month-old son... growl! Now when I say growl, I mean growl like GRRRRRRRRR... a husky and meaningful GRRRRRRR that is aimed at people or at any disobedient toy that dare cross my son's path.

It was like any other weekend in our household except for one major difference, my wife was away for the weekend and it was up to me to hold the fort and raise our son for the next two days. Initially I had no problem with this as my son is normally a mild mannered well behaved average six-month-old baby. Yes, it was going to be hard doing everything on my own and I was going to be exhausted by the end of each day, but it would be fun spending quality time with my boy. Little did I know how things were about to pan out.

It wasn't until Sunday afternoon when I started to reflect on what had happened over the weekend and more importantly how I was going to tell my wife? Could I get away with "what do you mean he is now growling? He was doing that before I took over for the weekend!" after all shifting the blame had worked for me in the past. Anyway, I relived the weekend through my head and realised that there had been some definite signs that my son was on the turn.

Breakfast: There is nothing unusual about a fruity baby porridge for breakfast and he did eat it all, however he did insist on biting the tray of his highchair after every single mouthful. Was this the 'hunger' setting in?

Change times: Nappy changing has always been a bit of a spectacle in our household and nine times out of ten I would end up with his pee somewhere on my clothes – even if I wasn't the one changing him. This weekend he was more restless than usual, he squirmed so much it took near on ten minutes to get his nappy on. Well the squirming got to the point where he had turned on his front and I had his bare bum staring at my face whilst he 'nibbled' on the change mat. Normal behaviour, right?!

Comforting: My son used to love being picked up and cuddled and hopefully he still does but every time I picked him up this weekend he would bite my shoulder with uncontrollable force. You are probably thinking, he is teething and you may be right but just as I thought that, it happened. GRRRRRRR... he husked at me and admittedly at first I found it funny as I thought it was a one off, there wasn't much laughing after that.

Night time: Both Friday and Saturday night went well apart from being woken up by a dull tapping. I checked on my boy and there he was fast asleep but at the same time he was banging his head against the cot bars in an almost hypnotic rhythm. Again odd?!

Morning: I wasn't woken up by a cry or the sound of laughter but instead short sharp growls that were obviously directed at me as he peered between the bars of his cot.

But what could have caused this cannibalistic behavioural change? Was it my wife's fault for reading the Twilight series when she was pregnant? Maybe my son had subconsciously taken this in? Was he Team Jacob?! Could it be the way I sneezed? Had he interpreted my violent sneezing as me demonstrating my predatory prowess? Had it been that I had given him more chicken than usual and now he had an uncontrollable desire for meat? Maybe it was as a result of my over-dramatic bedtime reading of the Gruffalo?

I guess I am never going to know what triggered the growling and my efforts should now be spent concentrating on how to repeal or at best delay the change from taking over my son completely. As for my wife, she surprisingly hasn't said much and having reflected on this I am starting to wonder if she had expected this change and if in fact she is the woman I thought she was. If the pack is evolving then this may be my last post and all the 'fattening up' my wife has done to me over the years is about to pay off!

www.idads.co.uk

3DFitLife

The Think Tank for Next Generation Child Welfare/Development

4 October 2011

Sonic & Sega All Stars & The "Racer's Line"

Yesterday was a beautiful day. Not just because of the sun filled days. But because it was the end of a story... a 'happy' one. My young 'un and I are partial to a bit of Xbox 360. Now what with me working away a lot I don't get much time to practice. And, at seven, he is pretty damn good at the games we like to play. I'm talking about Dynasty Warriors and Sonic and Sega All Stars. It is the latter of which I speak today. You see I have been at home for a month now, in between jobs shall we say. And apart from catching up on the DIY and paperwork I have made time for a bit of video gaming. Not least because my boy had been kicking my ass.

Nonetheless, dad being dad, likes nothing better than a challenge even if it is against a seven year old! Sonic got rinsed in the pursuit of that edge to get one over on my boy. A week later it worked a treat and I started whooping my boy. 4-2 was the score. It is at this point that I normally take my foot off the pedal and let him win a few but no I thought "let's see how he handles it" I said and proceeded to meat out a 5-3 victory too.

It became obvious that he liked to weave across the road a lot reducing his straight line speed and that he did not understand the concept of the 'driver's line' – the quickest distance around the track. Now the weaving would be easy to explain so I chose not to tell him and see if he could figure it out. But the driver's line presented a bigger challenge for me – how do you explain it to a seven year old when the tracks are irregular shapes? Do I really want to exacerbate his growing frustration by explaining something even I would struggle to explain to another adult? I kept quiet!

My boy doesn't like to lose so after my hot streak he decided we should switch to another of his favourite games – Bakugan Battle Brawlers, something he regularly whoops my ass at. Not my kind of game at all but in my current gaming form I did the unthinkable and figured out what the hell was going on with that game and started beating him at that too. His frustration was palpable and, yes, it hurts me.

But I felt the need to persist with my form and see how this played out, could he make a comeback? At some point I felt I would have to relent but on the other hand could he figure it out? The next day I asked Skig if he wanted to play and he said "maybe later". Later never came that day so I'm thinking the next time we play I'm gonna' have to let him win.

The next morning I was woken by his request to play on the Xbox. "Course you can" said a relief-filled dad! I came down to find him practicing Sonic and smiled. "Do you want to see if you can beat daddy?" I said. "No" he said. "Oh" I said to myself and on he played, stopping only to have breakfast and change the game so he could practice Bakugan.

The following day I decided to indulge in a bit of single-player Sonic and then Skig shows up. A sure fire way to get him to play is if I'm already playing. He is always happy to show me how good he is by beating the games' CPU player. But what about beating me? "Do you want to play me?" I said. He paused for a moment and said "Yes". My plan? To beat him in the first race then let him stage a comeback. A great way to teach the "getting up" part of life I think. Unfortunately, things didn't go to plan. I lost the first game – shocked I was. In my mind I thought "he won't repeat it." He did! And again.

And yet that wasn't the impressive thing about it. It was the style of victory which did it. No weaving all over the track so there were no easy wins for me. What was more impressive was his grasp of the driver's line. Not only could I not get past him, but his driver's line was better than mine! He was becoming increasingly difficult to keep up with! 6-2 that game ended! I asked him how he manage to get so good? He said "I watched you Daddy".

So what did I learn? That, given time and patience, kids can figure it out for themselves without any real need to ease up on them. That not only do they have the propensity to get over defeat but also the fear of defeat. I could have saved him the pain but then would that be living? At least he gets the complete experience in a safe environment. Time to get some practice in while I can!

www.3dfitlife.com

Floydsdad

Husband, father of two girls, and an idiot spaniel.

7 May 2011

Floydsdad in Padstow

There is something addictive about going crabbing with the youngest. She loves it so much. We have done it on an almost-daily basis on each of the three visits we have made to Padstow. I must enjoy it too, as I can't think of anything else that would drive me to force myself out of bed at 5.30 am to go and spend an hour in a refrigerated wind tunnel cutting up chunks of rotten fish, stabbing myself at least twice with the hook and tying myself up with 50 feet of twine on a regular basis.

I am guessing that crabs are not that intelligent, as there is no particular skill involved in hoisting them out of the harbour. This one, however, was as cunning as a fox. It had clearly worked out what happens when you stumble across a chunk of mackerel with a string attached to it and had developed the art of turning over as it was lifted from the water, deftly grabbing a chunk of fish with one pincer, whilst giving the crab equivalent of 'two fingers' with the other one, before releasing it's grip and laughing as only crabs can, as it dropping back into the sea. Today however, it had failed to bargain for the perseverance of the youngest, who finally lowered it bucket-wards to the bemusement of the staff at Chough's Bakery, who were treated to the sight of a middle aged man moon-walking along the quayside and punching the air.

After a quick hearty breakfast of a pasty from Chough's (I sent the youngest in as I had shown myself up somewhat!) we returned to the harbour at 11, where we boarded the 'Celtic Warrior'. Shane the skipper informed us that four guests had cancelled due to the weather forecast. Unfortunately, he told us about 30 seconds before we left the estuary and entered the sea proper. Someone told me that mackerel fishing was easy. This may be the case on a duck-pond-flat sea with the sun beating down, and a gentle willow the wisp of a breeze tickling the T-shirt. Today, however, I had to remaster the art of standing up, then standing still and then standing up again facing the right way. This took me around 20 minutes. The three other guests were girls on a half term break from University and they hadn't factored in the swell when ordering their final round of Jägerbombs the previous night, they gave up much earlier than me and hung over the edge of the boat making a noise similar to that you would make if you strapped on an industrial strength 'Slendertone' belt, and whacked it on full!

Needless to say, as we returned wearily to shore out of the eight fish that were landed, I had my name on one, the trio of students had one (which Shane caught) and the youngest hauled in six. This included a 10-minute stint where she put her rod down to mock me and then help me untangle my line on more than one occasion. At one point I yelped "I've got a monster!" and reeled in furiously, pulling against what seemed like a beast. The harder I pulled, the harder it pulled back. Eventually my excitement dwindled when I turned to face Shane to find him pulling equally furiously on one of the other guest's rods and shouting at me to "Stop winding man!" Another partial success!

We divided up the catch so that everyone had a fish, and after a celebratory Tribute or three in the Harbour Inn, returned to the flat. Here, the youngest amazed me by taking the knife and, with very little instruction and no sign of being squeamish, gutted, filleted, cooked and ate them both. She proclaimed it to be the 'best thing ever', and this fella's eyes filled up at the sight of the look on her face. A truly memorable day.

www.floydsdad.info

MrTheKidd

I am seven years married and a father of two amazing children. I am a Bible-believing Christian and a committed member of my local Church. I am the oldest child of five and a proper South Londoner, even if I do pronounce most of my Ts. Aside from Jesus, the main person in my life is my breathtaking wife who is my endless source of encouragement.

25 October 2011

The hated age

This post is a reaction to a bus journey I recently completed. I'm very aware it may cause another reaction. So be it. Let's set the scene; morning rush hour in a busy part of South London, the bus is getting full very quickly with a mixture of commuters and school children of varying ages. There is one mum with a baby and another has just gotten on with what looks like a five and three year old, doing the school run. All of these passengers are perfectly entitled to be on the bus as it is a public service. All of these people have chosen to board this bus.

Out of apparently nowhere (headphones in, not paying too much attention) the three-year-old girl starts kicking up a fuss, which quickly turns into a full-blown toddler tantrum. The mum is clearly flustered but doesn't respond with anger (hats off to you madam) but tries to soothe her daughter. This carries on for five to ten minutes. If people could be charged by the police for facial expressions, then there would have been a lot of murderers on the bus. The faces ranged from pure hatred that their journey was being disrupted, to pity, to looks that said the mother was doing a bad job. It very, very easy to spot those not used to being around small kids (although, that still isn't a guarantee you'd be sympathetic)

That whole scene should be acceptable in any situation; aeroplane, coach, train, restaurant, hotel; anywhere. It is a part of life that toddlers will kick-off; I did it, and no doubt you did too. And it usually doesn't end with childhood; how many adults whinge and moan and complain when things don't pan out to their exacting specifications? I can accept that certain places aren't suitable for young children, but where no such exclusion exists, why is the default expectation one that says 'Actually, I like the idea of children being seen and not heard'?

Children are a blessing – they enrich life, they help adults to grow in themselves and they give us boring grown-ups permission to have fun and play and explore. When was the last time you went to the park to have a swing or a slide for the sheer joy of it? When was the last time you marvelled at a snail or a flower? Just because we age and grow in understanding, doesn't mean that the world is any less marvellous. It would so us good to look at things with childlike eyes, with no expectations or cynicism. Why does our modern, forward thinking, progressive and ever (worryingly) tolerant society hate children?

PS – I have two children, a boy of five and a girl of three, so I totally understand the parent viewpoint. I don't hate you, so don't hate my kids for being kids. Thanks.

www.mrthekidd.wordpress.com

Diary of the Dad

I'm Tom; the little man is Dylan. Every week I share my musings about parenthood and the things that Dylan gets up to as he reaches each exciting new stage. I'm sure he'll grow up to find this embarrassing, so if you're his best mate reading this 20 odd years into the future, you should find some good material for your best man's speech somewhere on these pages.

6 November 2011

Your shout, Dylan

We took Dylan to a Christening last weekend. It was the first event of its sort that we've taken him to, mainly because it's the first thing that we've been invited to as a family – indeed, the bump that is laddo's little brother or sister was also included on the invitation, a nice touch – but we may have been hesitant beforehand due to his rather vocal nature. Like his old man, he enjoys the sound of his own voice. He also has a penchant for rooms that echo. Put these two together and there's an apparently irresistible urge to holler heartily.

Thankfully, our friends and their little lad didn't have their afternoon interrupted by Dylan's incredible lung power as he was a good boy. I have to confess that we considered leaving him with my parents as we were worried he wouldn't be quite so well behaved. Kate and I had to escort him from a parent and baby group once when his 'singing' earned us a few dirty looks from the established regulars. To be fair on him, he was joining in with Old Macdonald in the only way he knew how without the benefit of being able to talk yet.

I also had to take him out of the Early Learning Centre when he was clearly excited about what we were getting for his older cousin's birthday. A move that backfired when the part of the Arndale Centre I took him into proved even better for echoes. He was yelling his head off with a huge 'I know I'm making people look at you, Dad' grin on his face. Monkey! It's now his favourite part of the mall – just wait until he discovers that it's also the bit with the pick and mix stand! I understand what it is to have a favourite part of a shopping centre – the bit I like has HMV, Next, a sports shop that has a closing down sale every week yet has never ceased trading and, until recently, Game. Boom.

So anyway, I've been thinking of suitable forums for Dylan's shouting and there are a couple where he could be of great use. Now he can walk, I just need to modify the front door so he can open it – but not get outside, oh no, he's a keeper – so that he can shout at Jehovah's Witnesses – All Along the Watchtower eh Dylan?! – window salespeople and local Tory candidates when they don't get the message that we're not interested. By the same token, he will prove invaluable with cold callers on the phone. Here's how I envisage a typical exchange panning out:

Me: Hello?

Voice: Hello, am I talking to Mrs Hooker?

Me: What do you think?

Voice: Is that Mrs Hooker?

Me: No. I'm a man and there's nobody of that surname at this number.

Voice: Mrs Hooker please.

Me: No... there's no Mrs Hooker here. Have a nice day...

Voice: Are you the homeowner?

Me: Yes, but I'm not interested in anything you may wish to sell me, promote to me or otherwise extol the virtues of with the ultimate hope of me giving you my credit card details...

Voice: No, I'm not advertising anything. I'm just calling about insurance, do you have...

Me: Can you hang on a minute? I'll put our expert on...

Voice: No problem, Mrs Hooker.

Dylan: AAAAAAARRRRRRRRRRRRR! AAAAAAAARRRRRRRRRRRRRR! AAAAAAAARRRRRRRRRRRRRR!

Phone: Click, brrrrrrrrrrrrrrrrrrrrrrr

www.diaryofthedad.co.uk

Enjoyed this book?

Visit our online store (www.dotterelpress.com) for more high-quality, entertaining titles. All our books are designed to raise money for good causes. Please help us spread the word. You can review a book on Amazon, blog about it, tweet, include a link to it in your Facebook status or simply tell your friends about what you've read. Every little helps!

Forthcoming titles

If you've been inspired to start your own blog by what you've read here keep your eyes open for our new 'Beginner's Guide to Blogging' new for 2012:

A BEGINNER'S GUIDE TO BLOGGING (DOTTEREL PRESS, 2012)

Welcome to the world of blogging. There are currently around 150 million blogs on the internet and about 150,000 new blogs are created worldwide every day. That's about 1.4 blogs per second! Blogging is big and being part of it can be exciting, satisfying and – sometimes – financial rewarding.

But what is a blog? A blog, or 'weblog' is simply a type of website. It differs from other websites by typically being more dynamic – bloggers update their sites more frequently, sometimes daily or even more; blogs are interactive - readers often leave comments and create their own on-line discussions; and blogs are often multi-media platforms, featuring photos, videos, podcasts as well as text.

According to web analysts Technorati, two-thirds of bloggers worldwide are male and 65% are aged between 18-44. Bloggers are often more affluent and better educated than the general population – almost half have university degrees and a quarter enjoy household incomes of more than £50,000. While it's true that it is possible to claim blogging as your primary source of income (11% do) it's more likely that you'll want to do it first and foremost as a means of self-expression. To engage with others with similar views or interests or to attract attention to a craft, hobby or business venture.

Of course, of the hundreds of thousands of blogs being created, adding to the many millions already out there, a substantial proportion is abandoned due to lack of interest, lack of readers or – probably – both. This book will talk you through the process of creating a blog that will last as well as get and keep readers. You'll be invited to analyse your blogging motivation, decide what your blogging niche is as well as where to find your inspiration; you'll be encouraged to research similar blogs in your field, long before hitting the 'publish' button yourself and to slowly build your online presence; you'll be taken step-by-step through the process of deciding which blogging platform to use as well as choosing a template and building a blog list. In short, everything you need to know to get started as a blogger and to grow is here.

CONTENTS

1. *Why Blog?*
   What is a 'blog' and how does blogging work? What kind of people blog, and what kinds of things do they write? Is blogging for me? Setting goals and deciding limits before you begin.

2. *Blogging platforms*
   How to create and maintain a blog of your own in five easy steps; choosing the right platform (e.g. Blogger, Wordpress, Typepad); publishing your first post.

3. *Content*
   What should you write about? How often should you write? Do you need a blogging niche or can you write whatever takes your fancy? Individual and team blogging; review opportunities and sponsored posts; sub-editing your content; responding to comments.

4. *Uploading videos and pictures*
   File conversions and extensions; using YouTube; editing your video, including titles and adding music;

5. *Customising your blog*
   Changing and editing your template; using HTML; using the side-bar; adding gadgets and other features; using your own domain; third-part comment applications

6. *Making money from blogging*
   How can you get paid to blog? Should you carry adverts on your site? And if so, for what? Google AdSense explained.

7. *Copyright and legal issues*
   What every blogger needs to know about copyright, libel and contempt as well as tax issues, honesty, integrity and disclosure.

8. *Growing a readership*
   How to grow and sustain an audience, analyse what your readers like and what they don't and reach out to a wider range of potential followers. Using social media (Facebook, Twitter) to draw traffic to your blog; RSS Feeds; Networked Blogs and Email subscriptions.

9. *SEO analysis*
   The dark arts of search engine optimisation: making your blog 'visible' to search engines such as Bing and Google; Keyword analysis.

10. *After blogging – what next?*
    Is 'citizen journalism' a path to mainstream writing?

www.ingramcontent.com/pod-product-compliance
Lightning Source LLC
Chambersburg PA
CBHW051717040426
42446CB00008B/922